Then & Now

HORWICH

I would like to dedicate this book to the memory of the late John Smith, of Harts Houses, Horwich, fellow historian, advisor, and good friend for over thirty years, who died in December 2002. John gave up so much of his time to help individuals and organisations to research and understand the many varied aspects of the history of Horwich. John was well known for his lecture presentations to schools and organisations throughout the area, as well as his WEA classes in Horwich. He is sadly missed.

Horwich was known as a 'bleaching township' from the seventeenth century when many small 'crofts' had become established. During the eighteenth century, more cotton manufacturing was done in the community, which gave rise to some bleaching works being enlarged. In the 1790s, a new large bleach works complex called 'Wallsuches' was built by a family called Ridgeway. This works employed large numbers of local people. The works is shown here in 1925. Today the buildings are being converted into private dwellings.

Then & Now
HORWICH

JACK SMITH

TEMPUS

In 1884 the L&YRCo. purchased a large area of land in Horwich, on which a new locomotive building and repair works was erected, producing its first new steam locomotive in 1889. In this view of the works canteen from around 1910, note all the tea cans and wrapped bundles containing the men's meals on all the tables. The cans all have the 'L&YR' logo, for the Lancashire and Yorkshire Railway. The first steam locomotive built at Norwich Works, No. 1008, is preserved and can be seen in the National Railway Museum in York.

First published 2004

Tempus Publishing Limited
The Mill, Brimscombe Port,
Stroud, Gloucestershire, GL5 2QG
www.tempus-publishing.com

British Library Cataloguing in Publication Data.
A catalogue record for this book is available from the British Library.

ISBN 0 7524 3387 3

Typesetting and origination by Tempus Publishing Limited
Printed in Great Britain

CONTENTS

ACKNOWLEDGEMENTS

From boyhood days, I recall hearing stories from my father and his family, about 'old Horwich', although at that time, the stories were of little significance. Some of those stories helped me to understand a little of the history of Horwich. I must start my acknowledgements, therefore, with my father, Joseph Smith, his brother George Smith, and sisters Florrie (later married to Bill Corns) and Alice (later married to Jim Beresford), and their children, my cousins. My apprenticeship years at Horwich Locomotive Works led me to meet other life long friends who had an interest in the history of Horwich, the late Jack Rawlinson, and John Winstanley.

Their are many other former friends now deceased who contributed, one way or another, to my interest in Horwich and its past, either by walks, folklore tales, or by looking at old documents. Some of these were: Jack Charnock, Tom Crear, Tom Leach, the late John Smith and Mrs Evelyn Smith.

In addition to the above, I thank Mrs Margaret Rawlings, Mr and Mrs Tony Ratcliffe and the late Mrs Winnie Ratcliffe for her Horwich anecdotes, privately published, as well as Mrs Doris Aspinall and Chris Foley. I also thank Horwich Library and staff, and all the individuals who have allowed me access to their land to obtain photographs.

Finally, to all who have helped me in any way, thank you.

Above: During the First World War, Horwich Locomotive Works was largely dedicated to war work yet locomotive repairs continued, but at a reduced rate. A cartridge refurbishment shop was also set up. This was also the case in the second World War. The main output from the works during this time was the production of three types of Artillery Tanks, the Matilda, Centaur and Cruiser. In 1940, King George VI and Queen Elizabeth (the late Queen Mother), visited Horwich Works to see the tank assembly work, which was done in the Locomotive Erecting Shop. In this view, the Royal Party has walked along the platform at Horwich Station and about to enter their car for the short journey to the works.

INTRODUCTION

When discussing the town of Horwich one can, if one is not careful, spend an inordinate amount of time discussing its best-known product and associated work to the exclusion of its other characteristics. For about eighty years the building and repairing of steam locomotives dominated life in the town, followed by a further twenty years when electric and diesel stock were repaired and built. But, apart from this very important work that was done in the town, there are many more facets to its history.

The town is built on a hillside, falling from the high moorlands to the east to flat agricultural land and a peat moss and to the west, an open valley, mainly used for grazing land, called Horwich Vale. Through the west-side valley, a railway was built in the 1830s linking Manchester via Bolton, Chorley and Preston, to Blackpool and the North. During the 1960s, the M61 motorway was built through the west side of the valley following a similar route to the railway.

A branch railway line was built to Horwich town from the main Manchester to Blackpool line at Blackrod, between Bolton and Chorley. The branch terminated at Horwich, a distance of some two miles or so. It was opened on St Valentine's Day 1870. The coming of a railway to Horwich was accelerated due to the large number of businessmen who wanted their goods moved out of the town by rail, and coal for their businesses brought from the coalfields of Lancashire in the Wigan Area to a new depot in Horwich.

During the nineteenth century, the industries of Horwich were mainly bleaching, a craft which had its origins locally a hundred years earlier. At the end of the eighteenth century a new 'state of the art' works for the purpose of bleaching was established by Mr John T. Ridgeway. This new works was started in 1775 and was called 'Wallsuches'. The new works was famous for its introduction of the chemical bleaching process.

Some cotton manufacture was done in the township, which had its origins in the domestic trade at first, becoming part of the 'factory system' when small mills were later set up, driven by the abundant water power hereabouts. In the nineteenth and twentieth centuries, modern mills were built for weaving and most of the cotton yarn was brought from neighbouring Bolton mills.

Coal mining and stone quarrying were a part of the economy of Horwich from the eighteenth century, although the coal seams in the area were not of good quality. Also associated with the coal measure seams was a product called 'fireclay'. This too was mined and businesses started which used this clay to make pipes of many diameters, as well as all manner of connections, bends, traps, etc. which were used until the arrival of pitch fibre and plastic pipes. One such works was run by Messrs Crankshaw that was situated high on the hillside to the east of the town. Its works buzzer was quite famous for its distinctive sound and the works had the local nickname of 'The Klondyke'.

Another business in Horwich made sanitary ware. Here too, in the days before plastic, most bathroom and toilet fittings were made from ceramic material

A paper mill was started in 1862, which became Cooke and Nuttall's and several brick works were set up, in and around the village. A boom to these works came about when the new houses and streets were built for the new locomotive works' employees. The original township of Horwich consisted of houses and short streets built along the road from Bolton to the south, towards Chorley in the north. The road entered the village from Bolton alongside the moors to the east to drop down the hillside to the village itself, passing the parish church, built in 1831. Many of these houses date from the seventeenth century. This road was turnpiked in the 1760s.

The old road runs through the town along Church Street and Lee Lane, where the principal buildings are built, such as a Public Hall built in 1878 by Mr Peter Martin, later given to the town by Mr Martin's widow, after which it became the offices of the 'local board' and later still the council offices, as it remains today. A part of this building was used as the public library until a separate building was acquired.

The coming of the railway works in the 1880s saw much of the west side of the village becoming a 'building site', for, apart from the main repair workshops, their were also steel and iron foundries, a boiler shop, wheel shop, machine shop, paint shop, smithy, chain smithy, etc. plus 6 ½ miles of narrow gauge track and many further miles of standard gauge track.

New housing was needed for the workers, many of which came from the Manchester area, where the outdated former main works of the company had been. The company laid out roads and streets and built a large number of houses for employees. Interestingly, the houses differed, depending on if you were 'staff' or 'shop floor' worker. 'Staff' houses were built on higher land overlooking the works at a distance, whilst the 'shop floor' workers houses were built up to the boundary fence of the works.

New shops, churches and schools were built, as was a Cottage Hospital and a Railway Mechanics Institute (RMI), a recreation area was created with facilities for bowling, tennis, football and cricket, whilst within the RMI where, besides the educational facilities, a gymnasium and large ballroom with stage became the focal point of social life in Horwich. With the coming of the railway works, the old town also saw the building of a range of new shops.

Old pubs were enlarged or new ones built, in the anticipation of much increased business. Today many of those very big pubs are used as offices, flats, or shops. The railway works closed in 1983, but still functions in 2004 as 'Horwich Loco Industrial Estate'.

The town has grown considerably over the past twenty years, despite the works closure. Many new industries have been set up. A tram service from Bolton to Horwich came in 1900 and went in 1947. Today, talk of trams is on the cards again – for the future perhaps? Bolton Wanderers FC has built its new Reebok Stadium in Horwich and is often seen on television, with the former locomotive works buildings visible in the background. The old and the new are juxtaposed, yet Horwich still remains a 'small town' popular today as a commuter centre but still by choice, in Lancashire!

Jack Smith
July 2004

Chapter 1

SCHOLES BANK TO CROWN HOTEL

Approaching Horwich from the north, one passes through the parish of Anderton (Chorley Borough), in Lancashire. Close to the county and parish boundary was a pub called The Squirrel. Here we see a coach outing, probably enroute to the seaside in about 1920, which has stopped at the pub for refreshments.

Entering Horwich from the north, one crosses over the river Douglas, which is the boundary between Lancashire on the north side and Greater Manchester on the south, Horwich, side. The township on the north side of the river Douglas is Anderton, in Chorley Borough, where, since the nineteenth century, there has been a pub called The Squirrel, fairly close to the river. It was always a popular venue for Horwich people, only a short stroll down the hill from the town itself. In the 1960s the old pub was demolished and rebuilt on the car park a short distance from the original building. The old view shows the former pub and the new one, now a restaurant.

A short distance from the Squirrel pub, approaching Horwich, one passes the end of Dryfield Lane on the left. At this corner a stone cottage, for the resident waterworks engineer of the adjoining reservoirs and filter beds for Liverpool's water supply, was built during the nineteenth century. The old photograph shows a group of local ladies, believed to be from one of the churches in Horwich, who are having a day's outing in a wagonette called 'Favourite', supplied by Messrs B. Livesey of Horwich. The only man amongst the twenty-five or so ladies, and wearing a top hat, is the driver of the wagonette. In today's view at the same location, a group of boys on bikes appeared as I set up my camera, posing in front of the cottage, almost in the same place as the wagonette some eighty years before, *c.* 1910.

Looking uphill into Horwich from the end of Dryfield Lane there is a dual carriageway that was constructed during 1947. Previously it was only half this width occupying the left-hand and centre verge shown in today's picture. By comparing the roof above the modern 30 mph street sign (right-hand side), with that on the old view, it will be noted that there are projecting cottages to the right-hand side. These were known as Tottering Temple due to their once being used for religious services, and their falling into disrepair, hence the nickname. Also in the old view, note the roof ridge to the left of the tree and how that same ridge can be seen to be on the Crown Hotel in the distance, now visible because the old road has been doubled in width.

On the left of Scholes Bank dual carriageway is a road called Lever Park Avenue. This leads to the village of Rivington some two miles distant. Footpaths off this avenue lead to the high moorland to the east, including the famous viewpoint called Rivington Pike, which was one of the old warning beacons in Lancashire. It was used in the sixteenth century as a warning-beacon site when the Spanish Armada threatened. Lever Park itself was created by Lord Leverhulme, who had a hillside home with extensive gardens on the steep hillside on the edge of the moorland. The old view shows Lever Park Avenue. In the distance is Rivington Pike Hill, from where the Welsh and Lake District mountains can be seen, as well as the Derbyshire hills. Today, little has changed except for trees, plus two pylons erected at each side of the road to commemorate Lord Leverhulme's gift of the park to the general public.

A short distance along Lever Park Avenue, on the opposite side to Fearnhead Avenue (see photographs on p.15), is a pair of semi-detached houses. It's hard to believe that this rural setting was an area that saw bomb damage during the war years. Just opposite these two houses a bomb was dropped by a German plane. Other bombs fell on allotments close by at the same time. No-one was injured by the bombs, although several houses were damaged. It is said that the bombs were dropped here to get rid of them after a run over Manchester or Liverpool, but perhaps the bombs were intended for Horwich Locomotive Works which at the time was engaged on war work and building tanks. Today, the right-hand house of the pair that took most of the damage has an extension built onto it.

The need for additional houses in Horwich during the pre- and post-war years led to the building of several new council house estates such as in the Brazley area and here in Fearnhead Avenue. The houses were quite large and had gardens front and back. In the old photograph of the avenue, taken about 1950, note the absence of television aerials and the tall chimney in the centre, behind the houses. The chimney belonged to the pipe works of Messrs Crankshaw on the hillside above the avenue. The works used fireclay mined from the hillside for their products. In today's view, the tall chimney and works are gone, television aerials are on every house and cars line the street.

Rivington Pike has long had social and sporting associations for the people of Horwich. Although the parish of Rivington is now in Chorley Borough (Lancashire), and not in Horwich (Greater Manchester), 'The Pike' is closer to Horwich, and is a popular place to walk to. This is especially so on Good Fridays when the hillside and village of Rivington is traditionally thronged with people. The old photograph was taken on Good Friday and shows local people resting after the steep walk up the hill. A 'Pike Race' takes place annually, run from Horwich, to the top of the hill and back to Horwich. On top of the hill is a small tower, which was built in the eighteenth century by the local squire and was used by shooting parties on the moors. Today's view was taken in mid-June 2004, when the hilltop was almost devoid of walkers. The track has been re-routed and some landscaping done since the old picture was taken.

Returning to the Scholes Bank dual carriageway, on the left-hand side is a row of nineteenth-century stone cottages. The cottages fronted onto the one time main turnpike road between Bolton and Chorley, which passed through the original township of Horwich. The houses had long front gardens which may have been created for the cottagers so that they could be self-sufficient by growing their own produce. The old view shows these long gardens still in place, as they were until 1947, when the widening of the road for the dual carriageway, led to the shortening of them.

Another route into Horwich is from Wigan some eight miles to the west. A bus route from Wigan passes through Horwich Vale, a valley to the west of the town. Until the 1960s there were few businesses here, as most of the land was used for grazing or hay meadows. Only two large works were sited here, a bleach works run by Jolly and Jackson, and the other a paper mill run by Cooke and Nuttall. Both of these were in Star Lane. Today much of Horwich Vale is used for housing and many other new unitised businesses. The paper mill is now part demolished and the old bleach works totally removed. The old photograph from around 1920, shows men at the end of Star Lane after finishing work for the day at the bleach works. Today's view shows houses built in the field which, not long ago was a hay meadow adjoining Star Lane. Only the stone wall alongside the lane is unchanged in both views.

Passing through Horwich Vale, the road climbs uphill into Horwich via Crown Lane. On each side of this lane are long rows of stone-built, terraced houses. Some sections of the lane were not built up originally and had gaps in the rows. Today those spaces have been filled up with later brick-built houses. All the houses here have short front gardens with yards to the rear. Shops are few and far between in Crown Lane, at one time a Co-op shop was located half-way down the lane but is now closed. Both views here were taken as near as possible in the same place, where some of the changes include cars and aerials and the buildings themselves.

The dress of the children in the old picture suggests the date to be in the early 1900s.

At the end of Crown Lane is the Toll Bar Inn, located near the site of a toll-gate. Opposite the end of the lane is the side entrance of the Crown Hotel. To the left is the dual carriageway and there is a roundabout in front of the hotel, necessary today at this busy junction. It was to this point that a tram service from Bolton, began in 1900. There were two routes to 'Horwich Crown', one closed in 1907 when double tracks were laid on the other route. This double track was lifted in the late 1940s. The old view is taken from the end of Crown Lane looking across Crown Square where a tram waits at the terminus. The hotel itself is off the picture to the right. This photograph dates from 1938. To the right of the tram, above the bus in today's picture, the Queen's Head pub is visible.

Chapter 2

LEE LANE AREA

Behind the Public Hall, on Lee Lane, hidden from view by a wall, is a bowling green with its associated clubhouse. The location of this green is a surprise to many visitors who normally associate such greens with clubs, parks and recreation grounds. In the 1950s many pubs still had their own greens, but many of these had fallen into disuse by the late 1970s and early 1980s, often becoming car parks. Shown here are a group of bowlers in August 1934, posing for a photograph during playing a match between local organisations.

The Crown Hotel stands in a commanding position at the top of the dual carriageway when entering Horwich at its northern end. This large public house was originally a much smaller establishment, which was enlarged in the late 1880s, like so many other pubs in Horwich at the time. The front of the Crown Hotel once overlooked an open area called Crown Square where markets were held in the seventeenth and eighteenth centuries. In the nineteenth century a horse trough and an ornate gas lamp were built; the latter is seen in the old photograph dating from about 1900. This seems to have been a gathering place for men and children but where are the ladies? To the left of the pub is Lee Lane, the old road through the village, whilst to the right is Chorley New Road, which was much improved and acquired new shops and houses when the railway works came to the town.

Entering Lee Lane, with the Crown Hotel to the right, the old view here was taken between 1900 and 1907. The buildings are not changed a great deal, other than the cottages to the left, which stand well back from the road, where a more modern shop has been built at the nearest end of the row. The old photograph shows tram lines in the middle of the road (along with plenty of 'rose fertiliser'!), plus the support columns and wires of the overhead electricity supply. This tram route from Bolton turned off Chorley New Road and travelled via Victoria Road and Lee Lane to the Crown Hotel terminus. Another tram route was along Chorley New Road only, both of these routes originally had a single track. In the new photograph, to the right is a row of iron stumps blocking the entrance to an open area that was once used by Bolton Corporation buses between passenger schedules, after the tramcars ceased operation. Another bus terminus was sited at the end of Lever Park Avenue.

Along Lee Lane, most of the houses, shops, and pubs, as can be seen, are stone built. In the old picture a procession is passing by. It is celebrating the Coronation of King Edward VII in 1902. It is passing the end of Lord Street to the left. On the near corner is a pub called the Bowling Green. The cottages next to the pub were all shops in 1902 and today two of them survive. Note the tram tracks are in place. They must have been a hazard for narrow carriage wheels! In May 2004, when I was waiting for traffic to pass so that I could take the modern photograph, two riders on horseback passed me by. They were in almost the same place as the horses pulling the carriage in the old photograph!

Turning left into Lord Street around the corner by the Bowling Green pub, we see that some of the former cottages adjoining have been incorporated into an extension to the pub building itself. In the early nineteenth century these few stone cottages, close to the end of Lord Street, were the only ones in the street, beyond which a track led to farms, such as Ormston's and Old Lord's. Horwich races were held on land belonging to Old Lord's farm. Today, Lord Street runs into Green Lane as it climbs up the hill. On the left side (north), all the land is built up. In the old photograph, showing the end of Mary Street East, the Holy Trinity Mission church can be seen, from which the 1933 Walking Day procession of children with a banner has emerged. Today the site of the former 'iron church' is an open space at the end of Mary Street East at its junction with Lord Street.

Continuing our diversion from Lee Lane, along Lord Street and uphill along Green Lane, we pass the track leading to Old Lord's and Tigers Clough en-route to Ormston's farm. Here the old entrance into Crankshaw's pipe works can still be found, amid the willow copses. The former yard has been graded and houses cover part of the site once nicknamed 'The Klondyke'. Fireclay was mined and transported down to the works on a cable-hauled, narrow-gauge railway, which was always a great attraction for the local boys. We rode in the wagons across the fields until we got caught! In the works the clay was used to make pipes of all sizes. The entrance yard with its office, chimneys and circular kilns, plus the huge stacks of finished pipes are shown in the old photograph, dating from the 1970s. Today houses are built on part of the works site whose gardens will certainly yield a good crop of broken pipes for years to come!

Returning down Green Lane and Lord Street, we arrive once again at Lee Lane to continue our walk. On the corner of Lord Street, opposite the Bowling Green pub and until the late 1970s, stood a small shop. In its latter days fishing tackle was sold here. Note the gable end of a school is visible over the top of the old cottage. Following the clearance of old property on this corner, including the three cottages in Lord Street, the site was levelled to form a car park serving Lee Lane Congregational Chapel and adjoining day and Sunday school. The school building was sold for development in the late 1980s and has now become an Italian restaurant, shown in the modern photograph.

A little further along Lee Lane, we arrive at the building now used by the local council, the Public Hall as it was once called. The building was erected as the gift of Mr Peter Martin and is dated 1878. Mr Martin was a great advocate of healthy, social activities and the use of the building was to reflect this interest as a leisure and social activities centre where only soft drinks would be served. Following Mr Martin's death in 1879 his widow presented the building to the people of Horwich and part of the ground floor of the building was used as a public library. Next to the main building in Lee Lane were some cottages, now demolished. At the extreme left-hand side, is the wall around the bowling green. The old photograph dates from around 1905. Also visible to the far right on both photographs is part of the Independent Methodist Chapel of 1867 and school, now a nursing home. Compare the two photographs and note the 'clutter' on the footpaths with street lamps, bollards, fences, crossing/traffic lights, all of which we now accept as normal in our towns!

Turning to the right. while facing the Public Hall, we can look down towards the bend in Lee Lane and to the main shopping area in Horwich town centre, with shops on each side of a road, now difficult to cross were it not for the controlled crossing. The old photograph dates from the 1950s and shows, to the left, the front of the Public Hall and the Methodist Chapel and school, plus the later chapel of 1906, just past the old one. In the far distance is the parish church in Upper Church Street, a continuation of Lee Lane. There are several other small changes to be seen. Shopping out of town is now catered for with a new shopping complex adjoining the new football stadium for Bolton Wanderers in the Middlebrook area of Horwich.

Approaching the bend in Lee Lane, it is interesting to recall some of the old shops that used to be in this area, many of them in the same family ownership for generations. The top photograph shows some of the shops still there in the 1950s when this old photograph was taken. The Horwich Co-operative shop of 1902 is just visible to the right. Today the same building has several tenants, but the front pointed roof gable is still in place showing the Co-operative logo, – an elephant, carved in the stone. The row of shops to the left, which originally had three roof gables, now has only two. One car and a bus constitute the only traffic in the scene from the 1950s, which is so different from today, as the newer photograph proves. In the distance is the Saddle pub at the end of Browntow Road.

Chapter 3

WINTER HEY LANE

Winter Hey Lane links Lee Lane to Chorley New Road and is another of Horwich's shopping areas. Most of the side streets off Lee Lane, to the south side, used to accommodate businesses and some of them had access to rail sidings adjoining Horwich station goods yard. At each end of the lane were rebuilt pubs which catered for the employees at Horwich Works. They were the Craven Heifer and The Black Dog. Both have now closed as pubs and become shops, offices and flats. This picture was taken in Lee Lane in the 1930s and shows church leaders in a procession. Mr Hignett is amongst them (far left), wearing a top hat.

Winter Hey Lane runs from its junction with Lee Lane down to Chorley New Road at its lower end and represents one of the main shopping areas in Horwich. The view shown in the old photograph was taken from Lee Lane looking into Winter Hey Lane. The date is 1902 and the archway spanning the lane had been built to commemorate the Coronation of King Edward VII. The building of arches to celebrate important events was a commonplace thing in many counties during the late nineteenth and into the early twentieth century. Notice also the bunting crossing the lane beyond the arch. To the left, a projecting wall lamp bears the name of the Craven Heifer public house. It has now been converted into offices and a bookshop, with an annexe to the rear which is now a small bar, retaining a link with the past use of this building as one of the many Horwich pubs enlarged in the 1880/90s.

One of those businesses that had a rail connection at the rear of its premises off Winter Hey Lane, was Messrs Marsden, timber merchants. One access to the works was via St John Street. The old photograph, shown here was taken at the works during the First World War. The notice in the upper centre of the picture states 'Munition Workers employed by W. Marsden and Sons Ltd, Horwich, Lancashire'. The work that was done here, which needed so many workers, was the manufacture of boxes, of all shapes and sizes, mostly for carrying ammunition. Today all the old businesses in the area have gone, as also have the railway and station sidings. The distant trees in the modern view grow where railway lines used to be. The gable end at the very right edge of the old view, however, is also the one visible in the modern view, so not all has changed.

The old photograph here was taken about a quarter of the way down from the top of the lane, looking back to the junction with Lee Lane. The date is uncertain, but probably it is before the First World War. The buildings have changed little, as also have the shops, except that nowadays the window blinds are a little different. Notice how many of the shopkeepers have come to stand at their doorway whilst the picture was taken. On the left a street, which today has no name, had the name of Spring Gardens. Why did it lose its name? There don't seem to be any free-standing gas lamps on this lane, all being fixed to the front walls of the buildings. Unusually, even the chimney stacks and pots are in place on many of the buildings. Now the road is no longer cobbled, on the surface at least!

This is Emmett Street, another street off Winter Hey Lane, this time nearer to the bottom end of the lane itself. The old street that was, has now greatly changed. Some of the old property around here has been replaced with sanitised units which are surrounded by high security fences with lights and cameras. In the days when the old photograph was taken, there was not just a smithy in the street, but a wheelwright's shop as well. This was located close to the smithy, where the metal bands for carriage wheels and carts were made prior to fitting. The Fairclough family ran the smithy and the business dated from before the 1900s. Some of the products made, such as a cartwheel and horseshoes, seem to have been put on display for the purpose of the photograph. The location of the smithy was to the left of the wheelwright's, where the gable end building now stands in the modern photograph. The wheelwright's shop was on the land to the left, surrounded by fencing.

Near the bottom of the lane, for it is built on a gently sloping hill, is a row of terraced, stone cottages with gardens in front and some individual, detached dwellings. These stone houses were built during the early years of the street's development and were there when the locomotive works was being built in the 1880s. The detached house to the left in the old photograph, which dates from the late 1940s or early 1950s, was the home of Dr Sewell, a long-time family doctor in Horwich. The terraced, stone houses in the row to the left in the modern photograph still have their front gardens, the only gardens left in the lane nowadays.

At the bottom of Winter Hey Lane is Chorley New Road and crossing this will lead one into Mason Street. Today this is a very busy crossroads, controlled by traffic lights. Much of this area was developed in the 1880s following building works carried out by the Lancashire and Yorkshire Railway Company (L&YRCo.). On one of the corners of Winter Hey Lane with Chorley New Road was the Black Dog public house. It was one of those pubs that were enlarged in the 1880s and '90s. The old view here dates from around the 1930s, and is looking up Winter Hey Lane, with the side of the 'Dog' to the left. The pub is no more but the grand building survives having been fully refurbished as private accommodation. It's hard to believe now that it was ever a pub.

This is the last look at Winter Hey Lane, this time at the upper end and the opposite end to the Black Dog. The view is looking along Lee Lane with the Winter Hey Lane junction on the left-hand side. The old view is another that can be fairly well dated; as the old tram tracks are still in place it shows a scene from between 1901 and 1907. The photograph was taken looking along Lower Church Street, with Messrs Offord's plumbers shop to the right-hand side. Today, the former Offord's is still a plumbers' merchants. I can recall that Offord's used to have a flagpole at the front of the shop at roof height and on top of this was a kettle.

Horwich got its branch line and a railway station in the late 1860s. It ran from the main line connection at Blackrod station, some two miles or so distant. The branch had a regular service to and from Horwich, where the locomotive originally 'ran around' its train, for Horwich station was the end of the line. Later 'push-pull' locomotives were used on the branch until closure in the 1960s. The station had coal and goods yards and during the summer months ran excursion trains to distant holiday locations. In the photograph, a group of local people are setting off on their Wakes holidays and pose outside the waiting room at Horwich during the 1950s, while waiting for their train.

Chapter 4

LOWER CHURCH STREET AND HORWICH STATION

This view of Horwich station was taken during the early 1960s from the Lower Church Street end, where a ramp for passenger access remains today. The platform terminates by a set of buffers on three lines. The long platform and station buildings are to left of centre and at the end nearest to camera was the booking office, and the waiting room was in the middle of the buildings. There were station master and porters' offices. The train entering the station is not one of the normal branch 'push- pull' types, but is one of the regular service trains which ran from Bolton to Horwich. Today's view shows how the station was altered to become 'Old Station Park'. The cobbles in the foreground are a reminder of the former goods yard that used to be here.

In this view looking the other way, the station is to the right-hand side. To the left is a goods warehouse. Note the three tracks into the station itself, plus another into the warehouse. Above the warehouse, and more distant, is the station master's house, fronting onto Lower Church Street. This is the only building one can see from this location in the modern view, for trees now obscure the other buildings in this area. The view from today, however, allows the chimneys of the former station master's house to be seen.

From the railway station, a footpath ran through a narrow passageway, called Drinkwater Lane, to emerge on Chorley New Road, opposite the main gates of the Locomotive Works. It was used daily by hundreds of men coming to the works by train from distant towns around Lancashire. One passed over a small bridge en route through Drinkwater Lane. This was over a stream called Purl Brook, always a fast flowing stream, which was fed from the moorlands to the east of the town. The stream was used for driving mills in the eighteenth and nineteenth centuries. The course of this stream during the years of the railway occupation of this site could hardly be seen. But with the creation of a new park where the railway station and sidings used to be, the stream is now a feature again. The old view dates from about 1960 and the view today was taken in June 2004.

A royal visit to anyone's home town is always pretty special. This was the case when King George VI and Queen Elizabeth paid a visit to Horwich in 1940. In this view of the royal entourage, the procession of Daimler cars has emerged from the station, via the goods yard entrance onto Lower Church Street. In the royal car (in front of the Horwich Palace cinema) can be seen the King and Queen with hundreds of well wishers hoping to catch a glimpse of them. The royal party continued along this street, turned into Victoria Road and Ramsbottom Road, to Horwich Locomotive Works, where they had come to see army tank building in the Locomotive Erecting Shop. Notice that the old Palace cinema (where, when it rained you could hardly hear the film soundtrack) has been demolished. The cinema site is now occupied by Messrs Livesey's funeral parlour.

This pair of photographs was taken close to the location of the previous pair, in Lower Church Street, outside the former Palace cinema. This time the view is looking up the street instead of down, from the front of Gorton Cottage. The old photograph not only lets us see a general view up Church Street but there are several interesting details visible! One of these is the entrance arch to the ramp down to Horwich station. To the right, near the station entrance, is a notice board advertising trips by train. Opposite, on the left-hand side, is the canopy of the cinema. This scene with a procession underway suggests a date of 1929, according to the banner being carried

Gorton Fold is a group of cottages and former workplaces that date back to the eighteenth century, built on the old road from Bolton to Horwich. The terraced cottages are built in an 'L' shape configuration and are all private dwellings today. Gorton Fold played an important role in the Catholic history of Horwich, for in May of 1885, the first Catholic mass since the reformation took place here. Before that time mass was celebrated at Anderton Hall, a short distance from the Squirrel pub seen earlier. The old view is taken from a painting of Gorton Fold, which shows a large building to the left-hand side that is no longer there.

Moving up Church Street past the rebuilt and enlarged Bridge Inn on the corner of Bridge Street itself. In this street the water-powered Horwich Bleach works was an established firm from the eighteenth century. The works buildings are still in place but no longer used for bleaching. The buildings that comprised the old works can be seen on the present-day photograph. Perhaps the best-known business in Bridge Street was the Milner's Bridgefoot smithy, run from a building to the right as one turns into the street. The Calderbanks who also held the licence of the Bridge Inn operated the smithy before Milners. The smithy is believed to have opened in the eighteenth century and worked until the 1960s. In the old photograph, taken in 1888, staff at the smithy pose outside the former building which was demolished for road improvements in the mid-1960s.

Chapter 5

VICTORIA ROAD AND UPPER CHURCH STREET

In the years following the coming of the Lancashire and Yorkshire Railway Company Locomotive Works to Horwich in the mid-1880s there was an interesting influx of religious organisations. It was almost as if the 'new town' of Horwich, post-1885, was desperately in need of spiritual guidance! Several mission churches were established and others of a more temporary nature preached in tents or caravans. The Church Army was a regular visitor with a caravan, seen here, from which the good word was preached, and pamphlets handed out.

From the end of Bridge Street, this is a view looking towards Upper Church Street. The old picture gives us a good view into Upper Church Street itself, which, because of the trees, does not allow us such a good view today. The old view allows us to see the side of Victoria Methodist church, at the end of Victoria Road. Beyond the church are the police station, houses and shops that serve the local community of 'club houses' (an early home-buying scheme) that are in the streets to the right-hand side of Upper Church Street. Opposite the Methodist church and higher up the hill, the tower of Horwich parish church is clearly seen. In today's view from almost the same location, trees obscure much of the view, but the flag on top of Horwich parish church tower is visible.

Building of the Victoria Methodist church began in April 1887 (highlighting the fact that it was built 'post-locomotive works'), sited at the end of Victoria Road, an area developed by the Lancashire and Yorkshire Railway Company for its employees. The church was completed during 1888, costing £3,000 more than the original estimate, despite being built in one year. An adjacent school was built, with entry from Victoria Road, during 1890. The school hall was used for many social functions and concerts. In 1958 the church was used as a mortuary for the victims of the Winter Hill air crash when thirty-five persons were killed. In the early 1970s the church and school were demolished. All that remains of the buildings today is the stonework of the former boundary wall.

As mentioned above, Victoria Road was part of the 'new Horwich' built by the L&YRCo. in the 1880s and '90s. The road was originally to be called 'Jubilee Road' in honour of Queen Victoria. As the road was constructed in an elevated position overlooking the new works, the company built houses to take advantage of the hillside. This led to more senior employees being allocated houses at the top of the hill, whilst less senior employees had their houses adjoining the works boundary fence. The better and larger houses were called 'villas', and had individual names. The old view shows one of the larger houses along Victoria Road a short distance from the Church Street end. The view today is little changed.

Victoria Road was a tram route between 1900 and 1907, when a single track ran from Bolton to Horwich, turning off Chorley New Road, along Victoria Road then via Church Street and Lee Lane to the Crown Hotel, where the tram ran around the corner to join Chorley New Road again. It then continued along this road back towards Bolton. The Victoria Road route was lifted in 1901 when a double set of tracks was laid along Chorley New Road to the 'Crown Terminus'. Not many photographs of trams on the old route seem to exist but this view shows one of the open-top trains on Victoria Road, at the junction with what would become Stocks Park Drive, to the right of the modern photograph.

On the opposite side of Church Street to the parish church are rows of terraced cottages, many of which were hand-loom weavers' cottages, which today are private houses and shops. Behind the houses fronting onto Church Street itself, are several streets of largely stone-built houses, some of which date from the late 1790s. All of these form a community of cellar cottages, again usually termed 'weavers' cottages'. The streets contain many architectural features which can be seen nowhere else in Horwich. In this community in 1810, a small Methodist Chapel was built which later became a Pentecostal chapel known as the 'Aenon' chapel. This interesting building contained a gallery and decorated wooden archways and was closed in 1998. It was converted into a private house during 1999/2000.

Also in this community of houses with cellars, are some dating from the post-1800s to the twentieth century. In Wood Street, where a bowling green existed, a row of modern houses have been built, in keeping with their location, on a street which, on the opposite side, has three garden-fronted houses built in the mid-1800s. The date of the old photograph is uncertain but is likely to be from the early 1900s and shows three houses on the north side of Wood Street, Nos 22, 24 and 26. The photograph is believed to show the families who lived at the houses at the time. The houses shown in the old view are No. 22, to the right, and No. 24 in the centre. In the top photograph we see the three houses as they are today, with their twentieth-century embellishments!

Returning to Church Street, after passing the parish church and schoolhouse, we come to the end of Mill Lane. This lane bears a name that is certainly no longer in keeping with its rural setting. Gone are all the mills that were served by this lane, including Wilderwood, Foxholes, and Hole Bottom, along with their workers' cottages and the waterwheels or steam engines. The water courses that powered them are still there, however, now much overgrown, or diverted underground. At Mill Lane end, until the later years of the twentieth century, an open field existed with views towards the distant hills, where fewer trees allowed an even better view. The old picture at the top of the page shows members of the Tomkinson family, with their dog, relaxing in the field. Mill Lane is to the left-hand side.

Chapter 6

CHORLEY OLD ROAD TO RIDGEMONT

The need for additional fresh water for domestic consumption had risen with the huge population increase after the building of the locomotive works. As the population gradually increased post-1920 and new town mains were laid, additional supplies to top-up the town's reservoir became necessary. This was done by boring to a depth of 300 ft initially at Tup Row quarry, by 'Top o'th' Such' cottages. Boring continued to a depth of 1,174 ft before a satisfactory quantity of water was found. The pumping station was built at Tup Row and was opened on 17 October 1926 by Cllr Harry Carter, the chairman of the Water Committee.

The photograph shows some of the dignitaries and officials who attended the opening ceremony.

The old photograph here shows a view of Mill Hole, to the lower right, with the road to Bridge Street and Mill Lane in front of it. This was the old main road through Horwich until the coming of the Turnpike Road. From Bridge Street the road ran behind the parish church, passing Mill Hole and out of Mill Lane to Fleet Street and onwards to Higher Barn and The Crofters pub. In the distance is the large Wilderswood Mill built in the early nineteenth century. Above the roof of Mill Hole cottage can be seen the former cottages on Mill Hill. Note the cottages to the left of Wilderswood Mill; these are the only parts of the mill complex left today, surviving the 1911 demolition together with part of the outside wall of the mill building. Today's photograph shows a view of Mill House with part of the outside wall of the mill in the foreground with its blocked windows still visible.

This old view was taken opposite a terrace of stone cottages called Foxholes around the turn of the twentieth century. The children are by a wall that is still part of the wall to front gardens of these cottages, albeit across a lane. In the distance the upper part of Foxholes Farm is visible, many of the buildings associated with the farm are off to the left, at the end of the row of cottages here. The barn has now been converted to a private house at the end of the row. The Mason family held the farm and land here and the cottages were originally for agricultural workers. Mrs Mason was a descendant of the Willoughby family of Parham who later lived at Shaw Place, Heath Charnock. Foxholes used to be an isolated community and today new houses are built up to and beyond this single row of cottages.

Further along Chorley Old Road, one arrives at Ridgemont cemetery gates. The cemetery was consecrated in the 1920s. The entrance gates and the gate house were formerly the north entrance to the park of Ridgewood House. The gates were usually kept shut except for the entrance and exit of carriages to and from the Horwich direction to the main house, Ridgewood, about half-a-mile away. The projecting bay window at the front of the house, seen in the modern picture, was built so that the gatekeeper could see the gates and driveway in advance of a carriage approaching. The old photograph was probably taken in the early 1900s and shows a group of horses being led past the gates of the former Ridgemont Park entrance.

Inside Ridgemont cemetery, the original road towards the 'big house' itself is no long visible, this was lost when the cemetery was created out of the parkland surrounding Ridgemont House. A few years after the consecration of the cemetery the need for a small chapel became apparent. This led to the building of a multi-denominational chapel in around 1930. Changes in burial procedures during the 1960s and '70s, when 'chapels of rest' and 'funeral parlours' became more widespread, meant that cemetery chapels became redundant. By the early 1970s, this was the case at Ridgemont cemetery and a spate of vandalism accelerated the decision to demolish the building. The old view of the chapel dates from this time. Today's view shows the site of the former chapel.

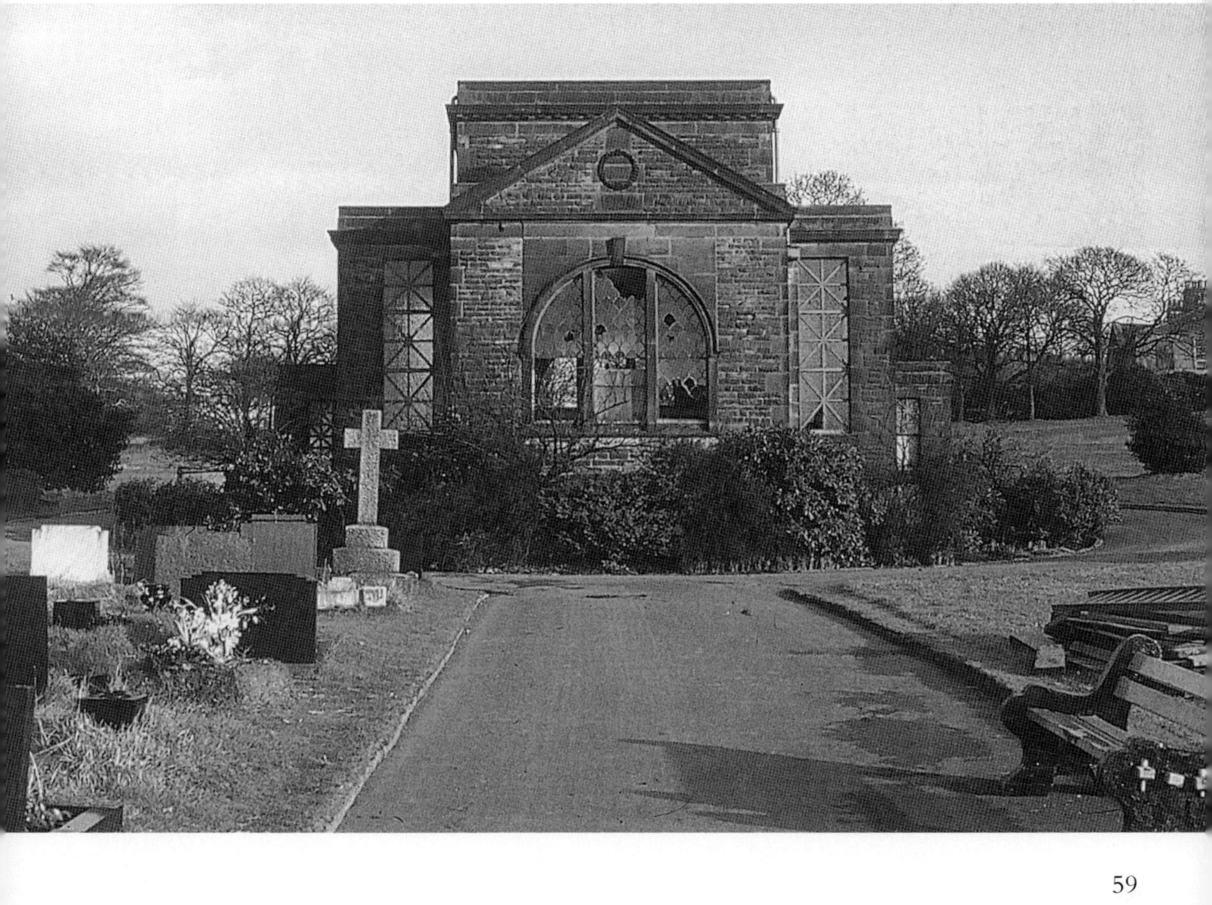

Ridgemont House is best known for its association with the Ridgeway family although it did in fact belong to another local family previously. The two brothers Thomas and John Ridgeway came to Horwich from Bolton in the mid-1770s after fire destroyed their bleaching works there. In Horwich they took out a lease at 'Wallsuches', where they developed the site for bleaching. At the time, the most prominent family in Horwich was Pilkington, who also owned houses known as The Stocks and the White House. In 1787 the Ridgeways bought both these houses and set about improving and enlarging the White House, at the same time changing its name to Ridgemont House. The old view shows the house in poor condition. Today, after refurbishment, the house is used as a Masonic Lodge and as a functions venue.

Ridgemont was a convenient house for the Ridgeways to live in because they were able to see, just across the turnpike road, their works at Wallsuches. There was even a footpath leading directly from the house to the works. In this old view, we look across Chorley Old Road, which was originally the Bolton to Chorley turnpike road, towards the Wallsuches works. Dominating the site is the five-floor Gingham House, to the left of the chimney, where much of the process work was done. To the right-hand side in the distance is Rivington Pike. In the modern view the works buildings are seen now much reduced in size and no longer used as a processing works. Bleach manufacture finished here in 1933. Today, these historic industrial buildings built by the Ridgeways (often called the 'Kings of Horwich') are being converted into private dwellings, in a new 'village complex', where it is hoped the Ridgeway family will be commemorated in some way.

Access to the former Wallsuches bleach works from the Bolton direction is via a lane near to Georges Lane end. This access lane passes alongside the far embankment of the water lodge shown on the previous page. Off the photograph to the right, are two rows of cottages in a three and nine configuration, dating from around the late eighteenth century, and once associated with the bleach works a short distance away. The cottages are called 'Top o'th' Such'. Some of the houses have been rebuilt, sometimes joining two into one, another was demolished then rebuilt and there has been one recent addition, retaining twelve in total. The old photograph dates from the early 1900s and shows the main row of nine cottages. Today, the buildings are mostly covered with creeper. The modern photograph was taken outside No. 6 (second from the far end in the old view), home of Mrs Bolton (left, holding an old photograph), with her neighbour Mrs Sharples.

Chapter 7

GEORGES LANE TO BOB'S SMITHY

The bleach works built by the Ridgeway family during the eighteenth century, called 'Wallsuches' almost warrants a history book in its own right. This group of men and boys were employees at the works and were photographed at around the turn of the twentieth century (find the only one smiling!). Note they are all wearing aprons as protection from what was likely to have been hazardous work. The former process building behind the group is, in 2004, being converted into private housing, ensuring the future of these historic buildings.

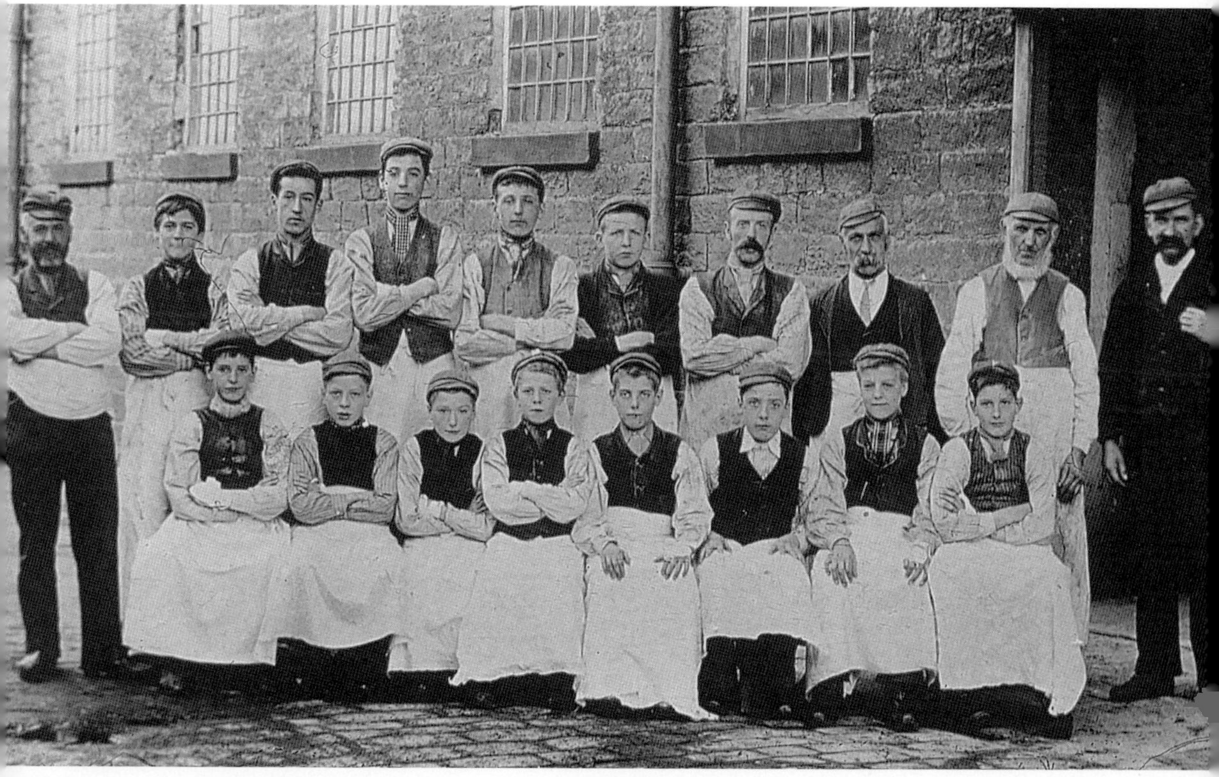

The end of Georges Lane is opposite the former 'Tup Row terrace, now replaced by a pub the, Jolly Crofters (a historical association with bleach crofts). Georges Lane leads to quarries, a former coalmine, to many farms and groups of cottages on the slopes of Horwich Moor. It also now leads to the Winter Hill television transmitting station. The old view, dating from the 1930s looks north along Georges Lane towards Rivington Pike in the distance and to the left is the enigmatic Rockhaven Castle, as it was called. Once the home of the Brownlow family from the mid-nineteenth century, in 1899, Lord Leverhulme of Rivington bought the house. It was demolished in 1942, due to its alleged 'siting point' for German bombers. Today's view shows how the landscape has been changed by the profusion of new trees.

The moorland edge on the east side of the township of Horwich overlooks Horwich Vale and westwards, to the seacoast. There were, and still are, many small farms over this area, plus small groups of cottages, associated with either farming and/or quarrying. Most of these buildings have been converted into private houses today, many of them with horses in the fields around them. In the old photograph, a row of cottages called 'Grundys' off Georges Lane command a wonderful view to the west, but their peace and quiet was disturbed with the coming and going of wagons passing to the quarry further up the hill. Today's view is little changed from the 1937 picture except, of course, for the arrival of television aerials.

The isolated location of New Chapel has its origins in the late seventeenth century, when local 'dissenters' gathered at one of their meeting houses. It is believed that the first true chapel was built on this site during the early eighteenth century, in around 1720. It is possible to observe in this photograph some of the changes it has seen over the years, from an original rectangular construction to the addition of east end extensions containing date stones, laid over the years, by some of the chapel's attendees. The bell turret seen in the1920s view was in itself an addition to the old building but it no longer features on the roof today.

A large house, off the beaten track, is Colemans, part of which was built during the seventeenth century of timber-frame construction. The house lies to the west side of Bolton Road about a mile beyond Georges Lane end. The driveway to the house, from the Horwich direction is some half mile or so in length and begins in the area called Bottom o' th' Moor, where a former small community of old houses has now been much developed. The stone-built gate lodge to 'Colemans' can be seen in the old photograph. Today's view illustrates how the attractive stone-built lodge can now hardly be seen due to the growth of trees and shrubs around it. Today it seems there is a growing desire for domestic privacy!

Close to Colemans was another grand house called Moor Platt. This was the home of the Haworth family. The Haworth's were formerly long-term employees of the Ridgeways' at the Wallsuches Bleach Works and later became partners in the company during the mid-nineteenth century. The new partners were Christopher and Charles Haworth who lived for a time at Wallsuches House which adjoined the works before moving to Moor Platt. A family descendant, Joseph Haworth was the last individual family owner of the works, selling the concern to the Bleachs Association during 1900. The old photograph shows Moor Platt house before it was badly damaged by fire and demolished. Some of the old stonework was saved and has now been incorporated into a new house built on the same site and shown in the modern photograph.

Almost opposite a gate-house and drive to Moor Platt house, is the hostelry called the Blundell Arms. Its location puts it just on the Horwich side of the boundary between Horwich and Bolton and is enjoyed by people from both communities. The Blundell Arms is not its original name; it was first called the Moor Gate Inn, because of its position on the moor's edge. The origin of the inn is thought to be eighteenth century following the setting up of the Doffcocker (Bolton) to Nightingales (Chorley) Turnpike Trust in the 1790s, when it became a stopping-off place for coaches. An inquest into the murder of George Henderson on the moors was held here in 1838. The old picture dates from the 1890s when the inn was looking somewhat run down. The new view shows the modern Blundell Arms with its attractive flower baskets and window box embellishments.

Bob's Smithy is another popular hostelry along the Horwich to Bolton road and, like the Blundell, is well used by both communities. Although it is only a short distance from Horwich it provides a good point to start a return back to the town via another route. The pub appears to have started life as an end-terraced stone cottage that became a beer house to serve travellers and local workers. The name intrigues many visitors, for the actual smithy that was located close by has now been demolished. The smithy building was actually across the road from the pub, at the corner of Chorley Old Road with Old Kiln Lane. The old photograph dates from the 1930s and shows the forge chimney to the left-hand side. Today's view shows how the location has changed due to road improvement and widening.

Chapter 8

FALL BIRCH TO LOCO WORKS GATES

Returning back to Horwich from Old Kiln Lane we pass along Chorley New Road. This was created as an alternative route between Horwich and Bolton in the early 1800s to eliminate the long steep hill on the existing main road past Horwich parish church that was turnpiked in 1763. Traffic on this lower road increased and was improved in 1824. Toll-bars were erected at the Bolton and Horwich ends of the improved road. The Horwich bar was just outside Horwich, in Lostock, referred to in 1824 as Little Bolton. The toll house itself was built at the end of Fall Birch Lane and is shown in this photograph prior to its incorporation into an adjoining house development.

The Bee Hive hotel is on the 'new road' from Bolton to Horwich and had its origins in the coaching era. After its 1890s rebuild, a canopy was incorporated over the entrance to the yard with its stables and coach house. The canopy was only removed in recent times following modifications to the building. The old photograph dating from the late 1880s or early 1890s, shows landlord Mr Calderbank (left) with his wife and five children. Today, the hotel has lost its stables and coach house and a new hotel has been built on the former yard. The hotel faces onto a busy roundabout with roads to Bolton, Horwich, Westhoughton and Wigan, a scene which could not have been imagined even a short time ago.

The recently developed area of Middlebrook is only just in Horwich and lies next to Lostock in Bolton. Until the early 1990s it was an area largely dedicated to agriculture with areas of land belonging to three farms. The approximate boundaries of Middlebrook are De Haviland Way to the south, Red Moss to the north, and the Bolton to Preston railway to the west. The east side was roughly aligned from the old Tesco site to Horwich Works. The new complex of Middlebrook Shopping Village, new railway station, and football stadium, are on land that less than twenty years ago was open fields, belonging to Sefton Fold Farm, which was built in 1666.

The old photograph shows agricultural work in progress on Sefton Fold land where today the new shopping complex and Bolton Wanderers' 'Reebok' football stadium stands.

Back on Chorley New Road heading towards Horwich, we pass a building that has seen many changes in its time. Today, The Swallowfield Hotel is a popular venue for functions such as birthdays and weddings. Due to its large proportions, it is hard to believe that it started life as a private house. It was originally the home of the Inghams, who, like many families in Horwich, were associated with the bleaching trade. The house was a long rectangular shape, with a central projecting front wing. That projection is still visible on today's photograph above the dark car in the centre. The house has been much extended towards the right-hand end and the left-hand wing incorporates much of the original house.

This is the Greenwood, a pub on the Chorley New Road. The original hostelry adjoined a small farm, a short way from the site of this new 1899 building extended to cope with the influx of trade when the railway works opened. The old building had a barn adjoining, to the left in the old photograph. The new Greenwood is a large building, which was decorated for the European Cup football tournament in 2004 when it was photographed.

Continuing into Horwich along Chorley New Road we come into the area that was developed in the 1880s and '90s, for the new workers at the locomotive works. The streets and houses for the workers are on both sides of the road. The names of the streets on the left recall the names of engineers. The old view, taken from a postcard, looks along towards a large imposing building on the right. This was the RMI, built by the L&YRCo., for the education and training of works apprentices in 1887/88. The original building was the one nearest to the camera with double doors. Another larger wing was added later (see opposite). The photograph dates from the late 1900s. Notice the double tram tracks, which were laid from 1907, and the open-top tram. Today's view illustrates the many changes that have occurred here.

We now look in the opposite direction to the previous photograph towards the Railway Mechanics Institute. The original 'Mechanics' can be seen in the distance at the extreme right-hand side. The centre portion and the wing nearest to the camera, running to the left, was the 'new wing' built in the mid-1890s. It was in this building that a large number of clubs and other leisure activities were established and educational facilities provided, making it a focal point in Horwich. It also incorporated a library and a gymnasium. The main function room could accommodate 900 seats and it had a large stage for plays and concerts. The later extension was badly damaged by fire in 1979 and although the original building only suffered smoke and other minor damage the whole building was demolished and has now been replaced by a housing development.

Opposite the RMI was the works canteen, built in the 1890s and customarily referred to as the 'Dining Room'. This building was close to the works' fence at the rear, and at the front, facing Chorley New Road and across from the 'mechanics', a rather special building was erected. This was called The L & Y Arms, but never had a licence for alcohol. It was built to provide accommodation for 'premium apprentices' and served as a hotel for them and visitors to the works. It later became one of the few places local folk could get a weekly bath, as opposed to using a tin bath in front of the living room fire! The old photograph shows the attractive front of this building. To the left is Gooch Street, where the middle gate into the works used to be. The L & Y Arms has been demolished leaving the former canteen. Next to the 'Dining Room' was a cottage hospital, built by the L&YRCo. to serve the new works.

The L&YRCo. not only built a new locomotive works, but streets, houses, shops, and even funded new churches and schools. A large area of land was also set aside to be used for recreational purposes with space for cricket and football. There was also open parkland with a bandstand, bowling greens and a wooden pavilion was built by the cricket pitch adjoining Ramsbottom Road. In 2004 the changes to this area of land set aside by the railway company are numerous. At the east end of this allocated site was a field used by Horwich RMI football team. Today that land is now built upon and the bandstand has gone but the bowling green and the cricket field remain. The original cricket pavilion is shown in the old photograph which, over the years, had become hard to maintain. A new pavilion was eventually built on the site and is shown in this June 2004 view.

The main gateway into Horwich Locomotive Works as it was in 1922. It shows the employees leaving the works at the end of the day. At this time the works employed over 4,000 people. Above the men coming up the main driveway, one can see the buildings of the main offices of the works. To the left of the men in the middle distance is the water tower and the gable end of the Erecting Shop. Furthest away, to the right of the driveway, is a fence which separated a large wood yard from the drive. To the right of the gate was a fence that extended to the Horwich Branch railway bridge. The fire station was built next to the gates here fifteen years later. Notice the tram tracks set in the cobbled roadway. Today's photograph shows the present driveway, offices and water tower but no main gates or gate lodge. The new fire station was built in 1997 and is visible to the right.

Chapter 9

CHORLEY NEW ROAD (FIRE STATION TO CROWN HOTEL)

The Horwich Locomotive Works was famous around the country as were other similar works such as those at Crewe and Derby. All of these works had their own fire departments to deal with workshop fires. At Horwich the works firemen also became responsible for putting out fires in the local community using their horse-drawn steam pump. By the 1920s a 'Fire Train' for the L&YR Co. was permanently stationed 'at the ready' in the works. This train covered an area from Manchester to Lancaster and from the coast to the Yorkshire Border. The train is seen here at the works approach alongside the Horwich Branch Line.

The developing 'village' of Horwich post-1880s and following the building of the locomotive works, brought with it a requirement for a more dedicated fire brigade to deal with fires in the local community. Initially horse-drawn steam pumps covered the immediate area, but later the need for more up-to-date pumps became necessary. The coming of the internal combustion vehicle married the two needs. The fire service at this stage was still one that was accommodated on 'the works'. The old photograph here shows a 1920s engine and crew in the works driveway by the main offices. I am uncertain as to what the cups were for which are on the side of the engine. In the modern view the crew look somewhat more at ease in their uniforms than the old firefighters did in theirs.

The works was 'home' to the local fire brigade until the first purpose-built fire station was built alongside the main entrance gates to the works during 1939. The fire train was still retained at the bottom of the main driveway and a fire office retained in the former works, 'check lodge', alongside the train. The 1939 station continued in use until 1996/97 when a new much enlarged station was built. Interestingly some of the stonework from the old station is incorporated into the new one, including the 1939 date stone. The old view was taken from Chorley New Road bridge looking towards the main gates of the works. Today the same view shows the new station and practice tower where, up to 1939, there was only a line of advertising hoardings.

Almost directly opposite Horwich fire station is the Chorley Road end of Drinkwater Lane. This old right of way ran from Horwich railway station where the lane joined the cobbled yard at the east end of the platform. The lane was improved from its rough track status in the 1860s when the railway came to Horwich. The upgrading became necessary to allow works employees to walk to their employment at the locomotive works from the station. It was a pedestrian way only after the 1860s and is thought to have been a carriageway or cart track before this time. The old photograph dates from the late 1950s. To the right above the fence, note the parish church tower, which looks like it is a part of Victoria Methodist Chapel, which is also visible. As is a set of goalposts at Horwich RMI's 'Grundy Hill' ground. Today the old route has become part of the footpath system in 'Old Station Park'.

Passing over Chorley New Road bridge and down the steep hill beyond we arrive at the crossroads of Mason Street and Winter Hey Lane with Chorley New Road. At the Mason Street corner until the late 1970s was the company of Messrs Pickup, sanitary ware manufacturers. Beyond Mason Street, the view along Chorley New Road, looking towards St Mary's church is shown in the old photograph, taken during the 1920s. The building with the roof level arch on the left side is another of Horwich's cinemas, this one known as the Picture House. At each side of the entrance was a shop. Most of the original frontage remains today although the roof level arch and other decorations have gone. The former cinema is now a children's play centre and a new cinema complex has been built at the Middlebrook Complex near the Reebok football stadium.

Directly across Chorley New Road from the previous photograph is a long row of shops and offices of two stories with roof gables. These buildings were also part of the development following arrival of the locomotive works. The old view from about 1950 will evoke some memories with local people, perhaps to recall getting a first bicycle from Penman's shop? There are many interesting features in the photograph; notice the uniformity of the roofs, the Black Dog pub and no traffic lights at the crossroads. To the right is the bridge over the railway and one of Pickup's chimneys is just visible. The old view was taken from the end of Rock Street. Today's view was taken in June 2004 and illustrates the many changes that have taken place at this location.

Some 300 or so yards further along Chorley New Road, on the same (east) side as the photograph on p. 86, we see an almost identically built parade of shops, also photographed in around 1950. This time the view is looking back down Chorley New Road towards the bridge over the railway. On the left in this view is a shop that will stimulate a few memories. It is the one with a large ice cream cone fastened to the wall! This was the shop of Ferretti's, who had an ice cream parlour here, and where some of us recall being told off for being too noisy by Mr Ferretti (I met and talked with him in July 2004), who is now retired. Also notice the mill lodge wall and the garage to the centre. Today the ice cream shop is an Italian Restaurant. There have been other changes in adjacent premises.

Through the chapters of this book we have taken an imaginary tour of Horwich along its main roads. There are many other places and views we could compare but for the present we return to where we started the tour. This old photograph was taken from almost opposite the ice cream shop referred to above and the date is in the early 1900s, The open-top tram, lettered 'N' for the Horwich route, is arriving at the Crown terminus from Bolton, and will have its catenary pole to the overhead wires turned to the other end of the tram so that it can run back to Bolton. Notice also the water trough in front of the Crown and the horse and trap emerging from Crown Lane to the left. In today's view is a Stagecoach double-decker bus which now serves the area along with several other bus companies.

Chapter 10

SOME SHOPS RECALLED

Horwich, even during the earlier twentieth century, supported a large number of rural houses and small communities, many of which were originally farming and/or industrial hamlets. These areas were served by trades people who had their premises in Horwich itself and made a thriving business by serving these outlying areas not supplied with shops. In earlier times Horwich shopkeepers used horses and carts to deliver to the district communities but with the coming of the petrol engine gradually most shopkeepers delivered to these customers by motor van. In this view we see the delivery van of Messrs George Pauling, baker and confectioner, of No. 88 Winter Hey Lane, Horwich, 'The Modern Bakery', on a delivery round. The date is in the late 1920s or early 1930s.

One could almost produce a similar book to this illustrating the many shops which have come and gone over the years. Thus we end this tour of Horwich by looking at just a few of those shops, starting on Scholes Bank where we started before. Few persons I interviewed could tell me about Messrs Wilkinson's shop at No. 12 Scholes Bank. The stone built property with an adjacent building has dressed stone frontages and random stone sides and back, suggesting an eighteenth-century origin or earlier. It may have been one of the houses built in this area in the 1760s when the Turnpike Road was made with a toll gate near the shop. It seems to have survived as a shop until the late 1960s and is now a private house.

Across the dual carriageway from Wilkinson's was another shop that seems to have started life as a cottage, like those either side of it. The shop was latterly called Cleworth's, and was well known for its fruit and fish products. This shop is another built from stone, like all the earlier properties along the turnpike road route and seems to have closed about 1979 or 1980, according to persons interviewed locally. It is now converted to a private house. It can be seen from the photograph that this house was a later addition to the property next door for its bricks are keyed into the original building. This property is the last one in Lee Lane as can be seen from sign over the door.

Further along Lee Lane, and almost opposite the Public Hall built in 1878, are Messrs Grimshaw's newsagents, another of those family-owned shops that are so well known in Horwich. The old photograph is from the 1950s or '60s and shows Mr Grimshaw at the door with a procession passing his shop. The procession was associated with the Holy Trinity Mission church in Lord Street. In today's photograph of the shop, which has changed very little, there is another Mr Grimshaw standing at the door.

The coming of the Co-op to Horwich is another subject of much interest. The movement began in a small way in a private house in Lee Lane during the early 1860s. The success of the shop led to a move to larger premises, which in turn also became too small. The 1890s saw the Co-op acquiring land and building houses. By 1902 land and property was purchased for clearance, so that new offices and a shop could be built at what was termed the Central Premises. The new building was topped off with a terracotta gable bearing an elephant, also cast in terracotta. The old photograph taken pre-1914 shows the shop staff in front of the Central Premises. In today's view the elephant and the 1902 date are still visible on the roof gable but now the building houses two separate businesses.

This is Lee Lane, close to the junction with Winter Hey Lane. This shop was called the XL Stores and was at No. 36. In the old view, the price cards on the footwear for sale in the window and by the door are all headed 'Wells Stock', at the top of the tickets. The date of the old photograph is early in the 1900s. This location has been subject to several changes and rebuilds over the past hundred years or so and today Nos 36, 38, 40 and 42 are all incorporated into one large DIY store. It has also been a supermarket in the past.

The north side of Winter Hey Lane has more stone-fronted buildings, some of which have seen many changes to their frontages over the years. Many of these shop fronts have been rebuilt to first-floor level and some have double fronts where there was a single one before. The old photograph shows the baby linen shop that was run by Mrs Pendlebury and who is standing at the door here with her children in about 1908. Today it is Greeley's butchers shop which has been serving the Horwich community now for some eighty-five years.

Other local titles published by Tempus

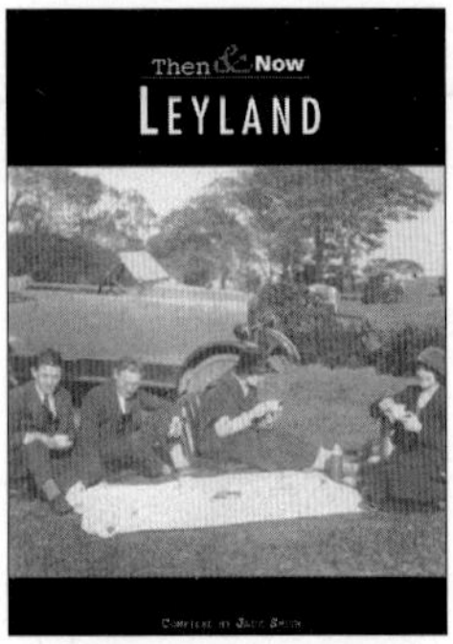

Leyland Then & Now
JACK SMITH

Leyland is a town with a name that is known worldwide because it is the home of some of the famous products, namely Leyland Motors and the former Leyland Paints. This book is a collection of fascinating old photographs, each matched with a modern one, to give the reader an impression of how Leyland has changed over the years.

0 7524 2672 9

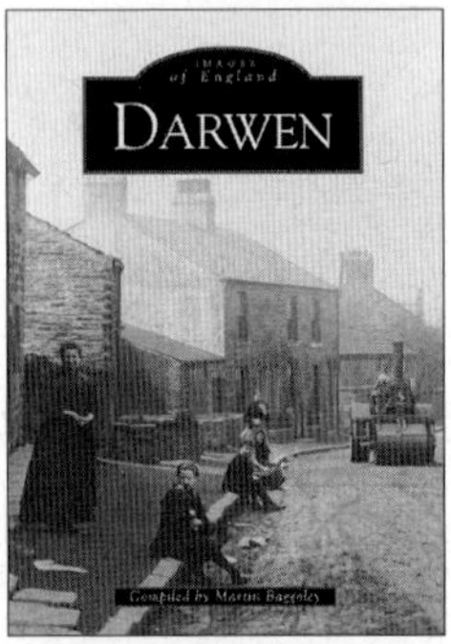

Darwen
MARTIN BAGGOLEY

This fascinating collection of over 200 old photographs depicts scenes, people and events from everyday life in and around Darwen. From images of Darwen at work, at school and at play, to those of the numerous mills that were once in business in the Darwen district, this book will delight all those who wish to take a nostalgic look at the area's past.

0 7524 3008 4

Atherton and Tyldesley
TONY ASHCROFT

Known locally as 'Bent' and 'Bongs', the neighbouring communities of Atherton and Tyldesley have witnessed a rapid growth in development from their origins as largely agricultural communities. This volume uses images from the Wigan Heritage Service to provide the reader with a glimpse into the past of this fascinating area.

0 7524 3048 3

Lancashire Coast Steamers
ANDREW GLADWELL

From the first Fleetwood steamers, to the *Waverley* and the *Balmoral* of today, the history of the myriad pleasure steamers that once served the Lancashire Coast is told here for the first time. Using over 200 images the reader is taken on a journey into Victorian seaside holidays and the steamers that conveyed happy passengers until the mid-twentieth century.

0 7524 2804 7

If you are interested in purchasing other books published by Tempus, or in case you have difficulty finding any Tempus books in your local bookshop, you can also place orders directly through our website

www.tempus-publishing.com